MYSTERY HUNTERS

ALIENS AND UFOs

Sarah Levete

Gareth Stevens PUBLISHING

Please visit our website, www.garethstevens.com.
For a free color catalog of all our high-quality books,
call toll free 1-800-542-2595 of fax 1-877-542-2596.

Cataloging-in-Publication Data
Names: Levete, Sarah.
Title: Aliens and UFOs / Sarah Levete.
Description: New York : Gareth Stevens, 2017. | Series: Mystery hunters | Includes index.
Identifiers: ISBN 9781482459920 (pbk.) | ISBN 9781482459944 (library bound) | ISBN 9781482459937 (6 pack)
Subjects: LCSH: Human-alien encounters--United States--Juvenile literature.| Unidentified flying objects--Sightings and encounters--United States--Juvenile literature.
Classification: LCC BF2050.L48 2017 | DDC 001.942--dc23

First Edition

Published in 2017 by
Gareth Stevens Publishing
111 East 14th Street, Suite 349
New York, NY 10003

Produced for Gareth Stevens by Calcium
Editors: Sarah Eason and Claudia Martin
Picture researcher: Rachel Blount
Designer: Emma DeBanks

Picture credits: Cover: Shutterstock: EKS bg, Faded Beauty r, Phil McDonald bl; Inside: NASA: ESA, the Hubble Heritage Team (STScI/AURA), J. Bell (ASU), and M. Wolff (Space Science Institute) 34, JPL-Caltech/MSSS 35; Shutterstock: Agsandrew 24–25bg, Anneka 24–25c, Artform 6bg(t), Bertie 40–41bg, Blueeyes 10–11bg, Andrey Burmakin 31c, M. Cornelius 18–19bg, CrackerClips Stock Media 23t, DK.samco 28–29bg, Esfera 34–35bg, Everett Historical 10b, 13b, Faded Beauty 1, Adam Fichna 15l, Fotos593 8–9bg, David Fowler 37r, Angela Harburn 38–39bg, Chris Harvey 42b, Nick Hawkes 26t, Edward Haylan 12–13bg, Steve Heap 18r, Iphoto 22–23bg, Jakub.it 8b, Jorisvo 6–7, Yuriy Kulik 4–5bg, Ladybird38 14–15bg, Lena_graphics 5r, Sean Locke Photography 38–39b, Aleks Melnik 25t, MWaits 22r, Ragma Images 43t, Elena Schweitzer 4t, Joel Shawn 16–17bg, SipaPhoto 40t, Solarseven 6–7bg, 17t, 19t, Talashow 28b, Tankist276 41t, Tilo G 26–27bg, 27b, Kenny Tong 36–37bg, Andrei Tudoran 20–21bg, Ursatii 42–43bg, Ververidis Vasilis 14b, Jarno Vladimir Zadvinskii 30–31bg, Gonzalez Zarraonandia 9r; Wikimedia Commons: Big Ear Radio Observatory and North American AstroPhysical Observatory (NAAPO) 36, Owen Byrne from Mountain View, USA 11c, ESO/E. Jehin 32–33bg, Geographer at English Wikipedia 30t, Gregors 29, J.S. Henrardi 16b, LA Times 12l, NASA 32r, NASA Ames/ W Stenze 33t, Olek95 6t, Drew Peacock 20–21, United States Geological Survey 21b, www.sprezzatura.it 7t, Taras Young 39r.

Printed in the United States of America

CPSIA compliance information: Batch #CW17GS: For further information contact Gareth Stevens, New York, New York at 1-800-542-2595.

CONTENTS

Chapter 1

STRANGE THINGS

One night, look up to the sky. In the darkness, you might be able to see the glimmering stars, spot the distant shapes of other planets, and the glow of the moon. But what else might exist in deep space? For centuries, humans have looked to the skies and wondered if life exists beyond Earth.

Stories or Sightings?

People have reported seeing flashing lights, spacecraft, and weird creatures in the skies above our planet. There are good explanations for some of these odd sights, but others are less easy to explain. **UFO**, or Unidentified Flying Object, is the term often used to describe an object or event in the skies for which there is no logical explanation. Aliens or **extraterrestrials** are the terms used to describe living beings from other planets.

There is an increase in UFO sightings after the release of movies about UFOs.

MYSTERY HUNTER

Look for the Mystery Hunter boxes throughout the book. They will ask you to consider the information given in each chapter and answer questions based on what you have read. Then turn to pages 44–45 to see if your answer is correct.

Reports of UFOs and aliens have fascinated people for a long time. Some people are convinced that UFOs exist and that aliens are watching us. Others believe the stories are made up. And some people enjoy making the question more confusing, by playing elaborate tricks and staging **hoaxes** to make it look as if there have been visits from aliens and their spacecraft.

Looking for Answers

Humans have always tried to figure out things for which there seems to be no simple explanation, such as comets in the sky or strange structures in the desert. Today, hard-to-explain things are sometimes explained as the work of aliens. In the past, they might have been explained as the work of the gods. It can take time to find out the real truth, and often there is no **conclusive** evidence.

Is the Truth Out There?

From glowing green aliens to flying saucers, the mysterious world of life beyond our planet causes much discussion and debate among the public as well as scientific experts, including **astronomers**. Read on to try to uncover the truth about extraterrestrials landing on Earth and glowing lights from alien **craft** lighting up our night skies.

No one knows for sure what aliens might look like. What do you imagine they are like?

A Look Back at Aliens

People have been reporting strange lights or craft in the skies for centuries. In the past, witnesses often thought they were seeing signs from the gods or the gods themselves. However, modern UFO-hunters think they were seeing aliens. Images drawn by people thousands of years ago and their descriptions do have similarities to modern descriptions of UFOs. We can examine the **evidence** of this in ancient writings and in images drawn on cave walls.

This hieroglyph from an ancient Egyptian temple seems to show a UFO-like shape.

Ancient Words

One example of what could have been an early sighting of UFOs took place in 74 BC. The ancient Roman writer Plutarch (c. AD 46–120) later wrote about what happened. He described strange events in the sky as the Roman army advanced on their enemy. He wrote: "With no apparent change of weather, but all on a sudden, the sky burst asunder [apart], and a huge, flame-like body was seen to fall between the two armies. In shape, it was most like a wine-jar and, in color, like molten silver."

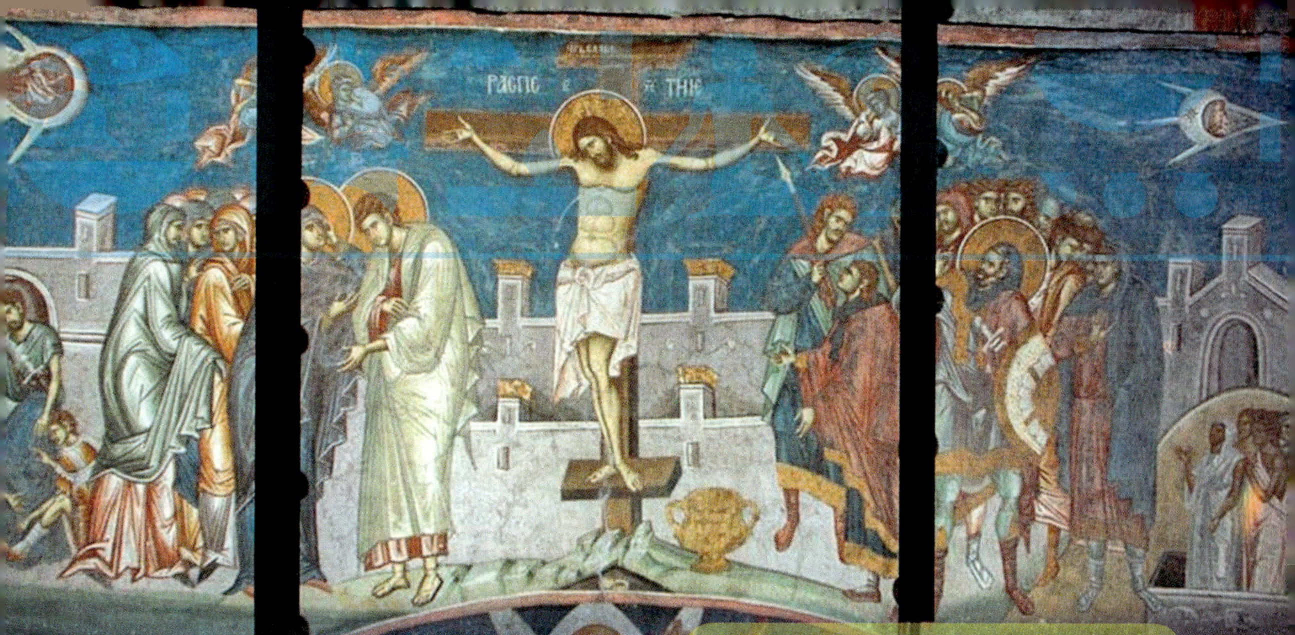

Are there UFOs at the top left and right of The Crucifixion*? Or was this the way the sun and moon were often depicted during the medieval period?*

Spaceman or Not?

Archaeologists found hieroglyphs (symbols) on walls in ancient Egyptian pyramids that look similar to UFOs. Many paintings and drawings of objects similar to modern photographs of UFOs were also made in the **medieval period**. For example, a fourteenth century painting called *The Crucifixion*, in the Visoki Decani monastery in Kosovo, Europe, seems to show two men riding in little spacecraft. Although UFO-hunters believe the painting shows aliens, art historians tell us that medieval artists often painted the sun and moon with human figures inside them, a little like small children often draw the sun with a smiley face! Many historians think the artist was not showing spacemen: he was showing the sun and moon.

MYSTERIOUS FACTS

Many people argue that happenings like those described by Plutarch were, in fact, astronomical events that we understand today but ancient societies did not:

- A meteorite is a fragment of rock or metal from space that hurtles into Earth's **atmosphere**. As it does so, it heats up and forms a fireball, which people often call a "shooting star."
- A comet is an icy, rocky object that orbits the sun. As it passes near the sun, it appears to have a tail of light.

The Nazca Lines

If you ever take a flight across the Nazca Desert in Peru, look down. You can see the shapes of animals and intricate patterns carved into the earth. Archaeologists say that these images, called geoglyphs, date from 200 BC–AD 600. They have remained almost unchanged because of the extremely dry and windless climate.

Dogs and Monkeys

The 700 images include the outlines of a dog, a hummingbird, a bird of prey called a condor, a monkey, and humans. Clear lines also create shapes such as triangles, spirals, and rectangles. These pictures are easiest to see from directly above, in an airplane. However, the lines can also be seen to some extent from the surrounding low hills. The Peruvian archaeologist Toribio Mejia Xesspe spotted the "Nazca Lines" in 1927 while hiking in the hills. Many people have studied these shapes and lines and wondered how and why they were made.

The hummingbird is about 310 feet (93 m) long.

How?

The largest figures are over 660 feet (200 m) across. The lines were created by scratching away the surface of reddish rock, revealing the whiter sand beneath. Archaeologists found the remains of wooden stakes in the ground at the ends of some lines. Was it possible for ancient local people to use such simple tools to create the beautiful artworks over an area of 190 square miles (500 sq km)?

Why?

What was the purpose of these images? The fact that the lines are best seen from above has led UFO-hunters to believe that they were landing strips for alien spacecraft, or messages to aliens. Some people think they were created by aliens themselves. Another **theory** is that they are related to astronomy, as a way of understanding the night sky. Many archaeologists believe that the lines were linked to religious rituals for finding water in the dry, barren desert.

This spider is best seen from an airplane. From the ground, it is impossible to see its perfect symmetry.

MYSTERY HUNTER

Consider the information you have read about the Nazca Lines. Do you think the Nazca Lines were created by humans or aliens? Justify your answer with historical evidence you have read in this book.

Chapter 2

MYSTERIOUS SKIES

During the 1940s and early 1950s, there were so many reports of strange things in the sky that the U.S. government employed a group of people to try to make sense of the situation. The group was named Project Blue Book. From 1947 to 1969, Project Blue Book recorded 12,618 sightings of UFOs. Many of these turned out to be IFOs—Identified Flying Objects!

Night Visions

On June 24, 1947, Kenneth Arnold was flying his private plane in Washington State. He reported seeing shiny objects in front of Mount Rainier. After his story was reported in a newspaper, hundreds more people said they had seen similar things that looked like "flying saucers."

This was only two years after the end of World War II (1939–1945). During the war, U.S. aircraft had often flown through the skies on enemy missions. After the war, there was much tension between the United States and the Soviet Union.

People were alarmed when they saw and heard military aircraft in the skies during and after World War II.

The U.S. government was concerned that the "flying saucers" could be Soviet planes. In 1948, Air Force officials set up an inquiry called Project Sign to find out more about the strange craft. This inquiry later became Project Blue Book. Its aim was to find evidence of UFOs and to figure out if they might represent a possible threat to the United States.

Close Encounters

Respected astronomer J. Allen Hynek (1910–1986) was employed by the Air Force to help with its inquiries. He was one of the first people to introduce a scientific approach to the investigation of UFOs. At first, Hynek was generally disbelieving of reports of aliens or UFOs, but his research led him to change his mind. Hynek developed a system to classify, or sort, the types of UFOs or unexplained sightings. He called it "Close Encounters." The term was later used for a 1977 movie about UFOs called *Close Encounters of the Third Kind.*

This is the model of a spaceship used in the movie Close Encounters of the Third Kind.

MYSTERIOUS FACTS

Hynek's Close Encounters system divided UFO sightings into groups:

- Close Encounters of the First Kind were when one or more UFOs were seen at a distance of 500 feet (152 m) or less.
- Close Encounters of the Second Kind were when a UFO sighting was linked with effects such as electrical interference.
- Close Encounters of the Third Kind were sightings when a living creature seemed to be piloting a UFO.
- Close Encounters of the Fourth Kind were when an alien was reported to have **abducted**, or taken, a human.

The Battle of Los Angeles

On December 7, 1941, during World War II, the Japanese bombed the U.S. Navy base at Pearl Harbor in Hawaii. Until this point, the United States had not entered the war. Now President Franklin D. Roosevelt (1882–1945) declared war on Japan and their ally Germany. Two months later, on February 23, 1942, a Japanese submarine attacked an oil refinery on the coast of California. Americans were fearful of an airplane attack. On February 24, 1942, citizens of Los Angeles panicked when they thought they saw Japanese aircraft flying overhead. The U.S. Army responded to the suspected raid by shooting more than a thousand shells (exploding devices) into the sky from antiaircraft guns. But the shells did not hit anything. No bombs were dropped on Los Angeles, and no evidence of enemy aircraft was ever discovered. What had the shells been aimed at?

*Could a **weather balloon** possibly be mistaken for a UFO?*

False Alarm

Los Angeles Times

Searchlights and Anti-aircraft Guns Comb Sky During Alarm

Many people believed the Los Angeles Times *photo showed a UFO above Los Angeles.*

The next day, the U.S. Army declared the "attack" a false alarm. Many people believe that a weather balloon had been mistaken for enemy aircraft. By 1940, the U.S. Weather Bureau was operating 35 weather balloons to measure the air pressure, temperature, and wind high in the atmosphere. Other people were convinced that a UFO started the alarm. Two days later, the *Los Angeles Times* newspaper printed a photograph that showed lights directed toward something in the sky during the "raid." Some people believed this was proof that a UFO had been circling the city. Others believed that the picture simply showed lights directed toward a smoky area and that the process of printing the photograph had made it look more sinister.

Foo Fighters

During World War II, many U.S. and UK fighter pilots returned from missions saying they had seen strange balls of light and other unexplained things alongside their planes. These objects became known as foo fighters. Some people think that the glowing objects were UFOs. Others believe they were secret weapons used by the Germans. Some scientists think they were a weather **phenomenon** called St. Elmo's fire, when a thunderstorm creates a lightning-like glow around an aircraft.

Pilots were under stress when they reported foo fighters.

The Lubbock Lights

On August 25, 1951, three professors from a college in Lubbock, Texas, were surprised to see lights whizzing past when they looked into the evening sky. There were more than 20 of these lights, as bright as stars but larger. The lights passed by in seconds, but the men saw them again on another evening.

The professors reported their sighting to the local newspaper. The newspaper published an article about their experience, along with photographs taken by another local man, Carl Hart. On August 30, Hart had managed to take photographs of about 20 white lights flying in a V shape. Lieutenant Edward Ruppelt, from Project Blue Book, visited Lubbock to investigate further.

There are often scientific reasons for lights in the sky, but many people believe in stranger explanations.

Conclusions

After taking down details of what the witnesses had seen, Ruppelt concluded that the lights were not UFOs but plovers, which are common birds. Ruppelt's theory was that, as the birds flew, their undersides reflected the street lighting below. Many people disagreed with his conclusion. They believed that plovers would not have flown as fast as the reported lights, and that they fly in smaller groups. The lieutenant said that the "photos were never proven to be a hoax, but neither were they proven to be genuine."

Not everyone believes plovers were responsible for the Lubbock lights.

MYSTERIOUS FACTS

When considering UFO sightings, it is worth keeping in mind some facts about how we see lights and moving objects:

- It is not easy to figure out accurately the size of an object in the sky without background objects to help.
- Reflections from clear glass or plastic, such as car windows, can distort points of light so they appear saucer-shaped.
- Lights in the distance sometimes seem to move, even though they are stationary. This is a common **optical illusion**.

Unsolved Mystery

Over a period of six months from November 1989, many people in Belgium, in Europe, reported strange spacecraft traveling across the skies. The reports began in the city of Liège. People saw triangle-shaped lights or objects hovering in the air. **Radar** picked up signs of something in the atmosphere. Radar is a system that uses **radio waves** to detect objects.

Call the F-16s

Belgian F-16 fighter planes were sent to investigate the reports of UFOs. On the ground, the radar operators noticed that the objects showing up on their screens disappeared when the fighters arrived in the area, but returned when they left. This continued for six months. No one was able to explain what people had seen, nor what the radar had detected.

"The mystery remains unresolved," wrote General Wilfried de Brouwer, Chief of Operations of the Belgian Air Staff. Could **electromagnetic interference** have been showing up on the radar? General de Brouwer wrote there was no proof of that. "Eyewitnesses ... stated that the bright spots they were observing lost their intensity as the F-16s approached or were even extinguished completely.... At all events, the Air Force has arrived at the conclusion that a number of abnormal phenomena have occurred in Belgian airspace." The authorities decided the sightings were due to a "number of unauthorized air activities." In other words, they thought people were secretly flying some form of craft, then hiding when the Air Force arrived. Some people think the lights belonged to helicopters, whose engines could not be heard because of strong winds.

This photo was a fake, but did UFOs visit Belgium?

Evidence from radar reports supports some UFO sightings.

Explanations and Questions

The U.S. National Aeronautics and Space Administration (NASA) examined the only clear photograph of the Belgian lights. It was thought to be genuine until the photographer, known as Patrick M., admitted he had faked the image. So perhaps the sightings started as a hoax, and then others believed they really saw something, led on because so many other people believed it. But if this is the case, there remain unanswered questions. What was the radar detecting? Why would the lights disappear as the F-16s approached?

MYSTERY HUNTER

Based on the evidence you have read, do you think the lights in Belgium were UFOs or something else? What scientific explanations can you give to back up your answer?

Chapter 3

THE ALIENS HAVE LANDED

No one has ever proven that aliens have traveled to our planet—yet no one has ever proven that they have not. Although there have been many hoaxes and mistaken sightings, that does not mean that aliens are not among us right now, does it...?

Adamski Photos

From 1946 onward, George Adamski, who lived in California, claimed not just to witness countless UFOs, but also to photograph them and even travel in them. He said he communicated with the human-like aliens through telepathy (mind power) and hand gestures. Adamski became famous and wrote three very popular books about his experiences. However, when experts examined his photographs, they said they were fakes: the "UFOs" were constructed from light bulbs, gas lanterns, and a "chicken brooder."

This is just a light bulb, but it looks quite a lot like a UFO!

Fake or Real?

In 1950, Evelyn Trent claimed that she saw a strange flying craft over her farm in McMinnville, Oregon. She shouted to her husband, who grabbed a camera and took photos of the craft. Many UFO-believers are convinced that the McMinnville photos show a UFO visiting planet Earth. However, several experts who have examined the photos believe they can see a string: they think the "UFO" is a model dangling from a thread!

Are alien abductions just the stuff of movies?

Body of Bread

In April 2011, two students, Timur Hilall and Kirill Vlasov, said they had found the body of an alien lying in the snow in Siberia. They claimed that the alien was injured when a UFO crashed nearby. They shot a video of the body which was soon shared on the Internet 700,000 times. The alien turned out to be made of bread covered with chicken skin.

What to Believe?

You only have to look on the Internet to ready plenty of accounts of alien sightings across the world. The difficulty is in figuring out which ones may be based on fact, and which are deliberate hoaxes. How can people discover whether a sighting or report is a hoax or whether it might have a grain of truth? An investigator must gather as much evidence as possible and assemble all the facts. The investigator has to find evidence to back up the witness statements.

Roswell Daily Record

RAAF Captures Flying Saucer On Ranch in Roswell Region

Claims Army Is Stacking Courts Martial

House Passes Tax Slash by Large Margin

Security Council Paves Way to Talks On Arms Reductions

No Details of Flying Disk Are Revealed

Ex-King Carol Weds Mme. Lupescu

Some of Soviet Satellites May Attend Paris Meeting

Roswellians Have Differing Opinions On Flying Saucers

American League Wins All-Star Game

Miners and Operators Sign Highest Wage Pact in History

The Roswell Daily Record *set off a storm.*

The Secret Army Base

"RAAF Captures Flying Saucer On Ranch in Roswell Region." In July 1947, this **headline** about the Roswell Army Air Field (RAAF) in the *Roswell Daily Record* began one of the United States' most famous alien and UFO mysteries. Known as the Roswell Incident, it is still the cause of much debate.

During the 1940s, the U.S. Army Air Force had a base near the New Mexican town of Roswell. At this base, the army carried out top-secret tests and experiments, known as Project Mogul. They were trying to find out if the Soviet Union was testing **atomic bombs**. They did this by flying microphones on **surveillance** balloons very high in the atmosphere to detect **sound waves** if any such tests took place. The army kept the project secret for over 20 years. This secrecy made the mystery of the Roswell Incident even harder to unravel.

The Roswell Incident

In early July 1947, ranch worker William Brazell noticed some strange items scattered over the ranch where he worked. Brazell, who was interested in UFOs, was sure they were wreckage from a UFO. He told the local sheriff about what he had found. The sheriff told the army base. Soon army agents were at the ranch, collecting the **debris**.

The next day, a statement from the RAAF stated that a "flying disk" had crashed near Roswell. But then the RAAF changed their story. They said it was not a flying disk, but a weather balloon. Reporters who arrived at the ranch were shown debris said to be from the crash area, such as foil, rubber, and wood. These could have come from a weather balloon. In fact, many people think they came from a surveillance balloon, but that the U.S. Army did not want to admit that as it wanted to keep Project Mogul secret.

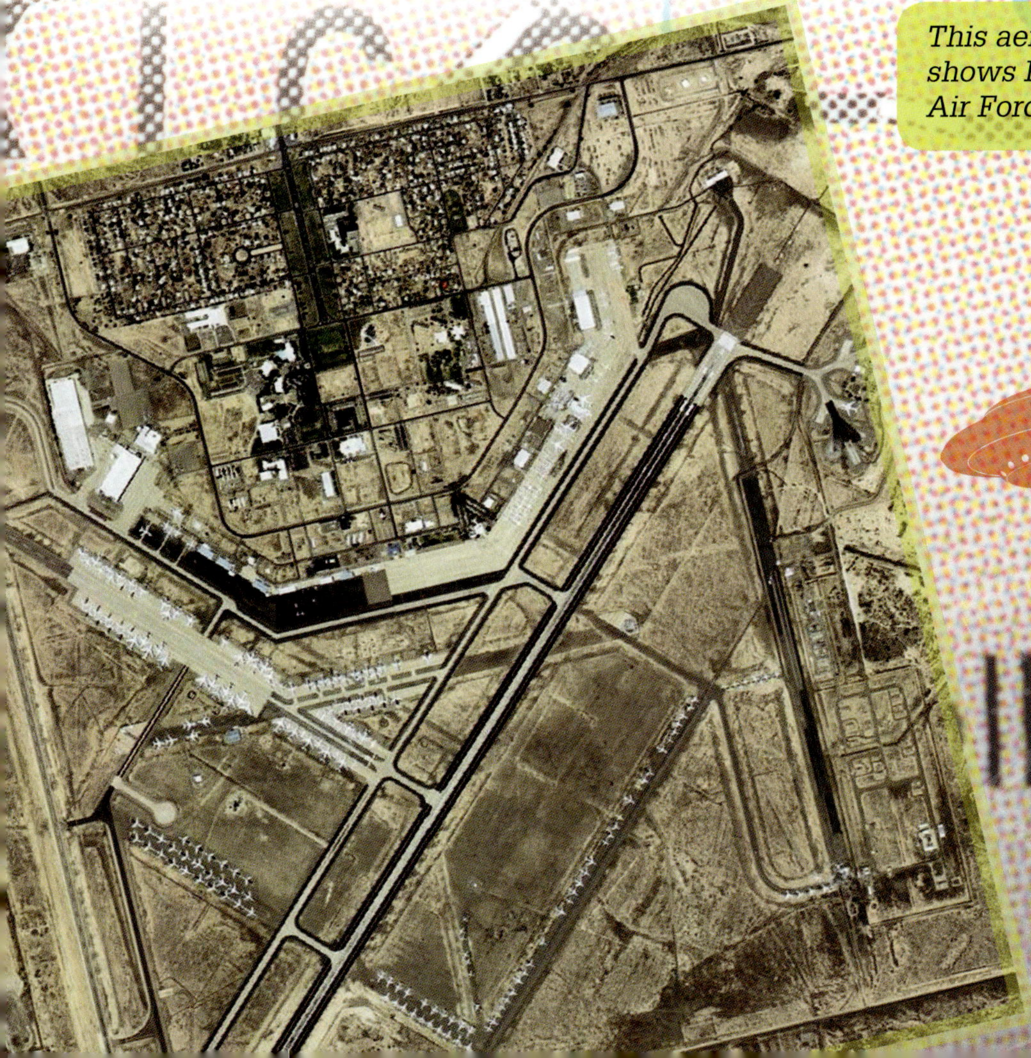

This aerial photo shows Roswell Air Force Base.

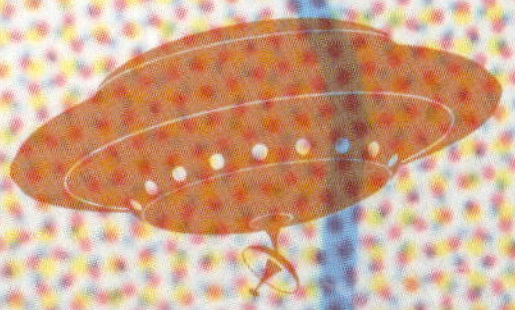

The Alien Autopsy

In 1989, over 40 years after the Roswell Incident, the story of the crashed "flying disk" became headline news again. It all started when a new witness came forward. This man, Glenn Dennis, claimed that a friend of his had worked at the Roswell army base as a nurse back in 1947. Dennis said the nurse had accidentally walked into a room where she saw doctors looking at three strange, dead creatures.

Not Human

Dennis said that these creatures were not human: they had small bodies, spindly arms, and huge bald heads. After him, many other people came forward to say they had seen UFOs and aliens near Roswell. Dennis's account proved to be so flawed that it was unbelievable, but by then many people were convinced that a spacecraft had crashed at Roswell, killing its alien pilots.

Today, many people visit Roswell and its UFO museum to find out more.

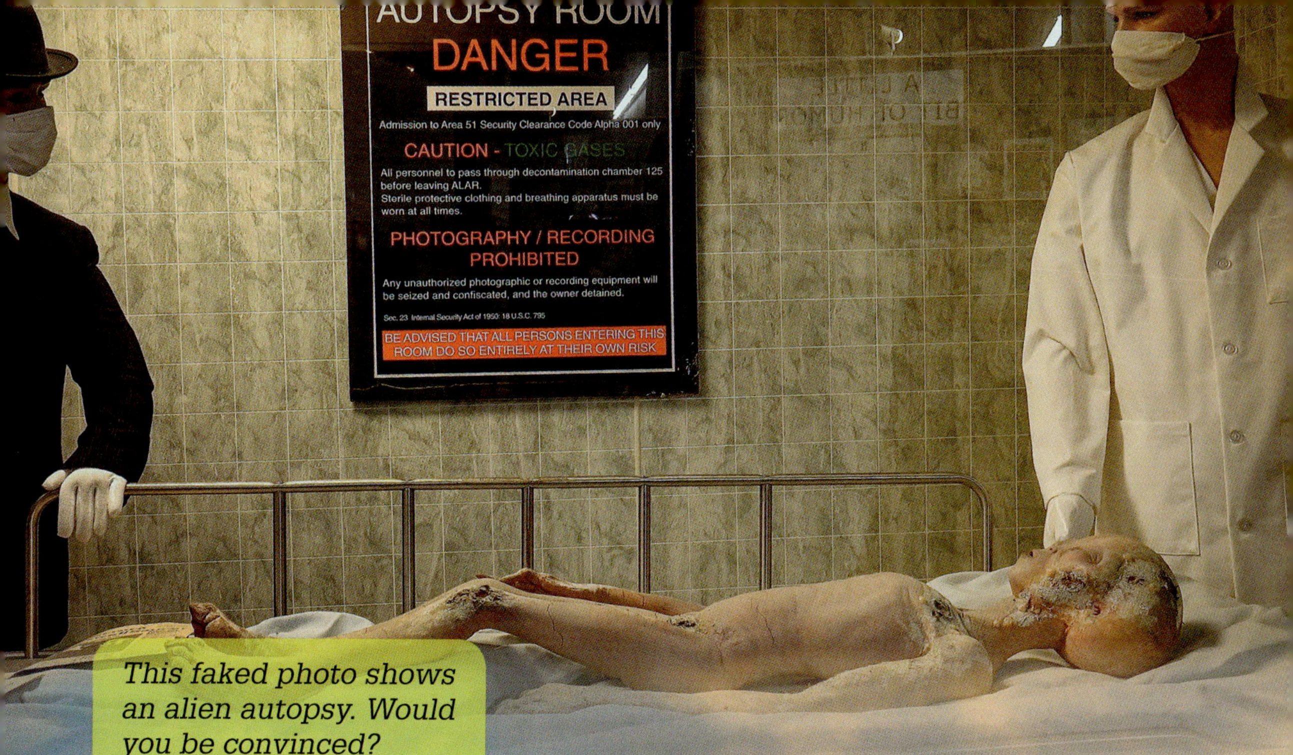

This faked photo shows an alien autopsy. Would you be convinced?

Documentary Evidence?

In May 1995, a British music and video producer, Ray Santilli, said he had film **footage** of doctors inspecting the bodies of the aliens that died at Roswell. Presented as a documentary (a film based on factual evidence), it was shown on the Fox TV network. In the footage, surgeons are seen cutting into the body of one of the aliens. Most people dismissed the film as a hoax. They pointed out that a real **autopsy**, a thorough investigation of a dead body, would take weeks, not a couple of hours. The image blurred every time it came close to the alien. The alien body looked as if it was made of rubber. Later, Santilli admitted the film was a hoax, but still claimed to have seen original footage of the incident!

MYSTERY HUNTER

Using the information you have read in this chapter, decide if you think there is enough scientific and historical evidence to prove that aliens crashed their spaceship at Roswell. Give reasons for your answer.

Looking Like Us

Little green men; large-headed, blue, bald figures; wobbly-shaped creatures—an alien could look like anything. Or could it? Professor Simon Conway Morris (born 1951) studies the way animals evolve, or develop over time. He says aliens may look more like humans than we expect. According to Morris's theory, different species are likely to evolve with similar features, especially if they exist on planets with similar environments to Earth.

Checking the Truth

Professor John E. Mack (1929–2004) was a psychiatrist, a doctor who treats and studies mental health problems. He became interested in reports of people who said they had been abducted by aliens. Mack carried out many tests on these "abductees." Although at first he assumed they were suffering from mental illness, he changed his opinion. He said the abduction phenomenon needed further investigation. He thought that the abductees' experiences were probably some sort of **vision**.

Aliens are often drawn with large eyes and balloon-shaped heads.

MYSTERIOUS FACTS

Some psychiatrists do not believe in alien abductions. They offer other explanations for what people may have experienced:

- Hallucinations are when someone sees or hears something that is not really there. Powerful hallucinations can happen when someone is half asleep, just before waking or as they fall asleep.
- "False memory" is when someone has memories of events that did not happen but which they believe are real. This is a fairly common phenomenon, caused by our imaginations and memories becoming mixed up.

Crop circles can be perfectly symmetrical, like this one.

Crop Circles

A crop circle is a mysterious shape or pattern marked out in fields where crops are grown. One of the first recorded crop circles appeared in 1966 in Australia. A farmer reported seeing a saucer-shaped craft rise 30 feet (12 m) from a swamp before flying off. The farmer went to investigate. He found a circular area 32 feet (10 m) long by 25 feet (8 m) wide. The grass had been flattened in clockwise curves, and reeds had been uprooted from the mud and laid flat.

Other, similar shapes were found nearby. They were named "saucer nests." The Royal Australian Air Force (RAAF) investigated. It concluded: "During enquiries a number of local residents stated that the reported 'nests' are fairly common during the onset of the 'wet' [season]." People explained that the shapes could have been created by **dust devils** or **waterspouts**. But that did not convince those who thought they were the work of aliens.

Watch the Crop

During the 1980s, in the United Kingdom, many farmers woke up to find their grain fields looked very different from the previous day. Overnight, circles, shapes, and patterns had been created by flattening part of the cereal crop. The patterns became known as crop circles. Many people believed these were the work of aliens.

In 1991, two men named Doug Bower and David Chorley admitted that they were responsible for 200 of the crop circles that had sprung up overnight in the United Kingdom. It was not clear who or what was responsible for the hundreds of other crop circles. To prove they were behind some of the circles, the two men demonstrated how to make them in front of journalists. These hoaxes and others like them have not stopped people from believing that smart aliens are responsible for these intricate crop circles. The study of crop circles even has its own scientific name, "cereology."

Fairy Circles

Viewed from above, the dry grasslands in Namibia, Africa, are marked with countless round patches where no grass or other plant grows. Known as fairy circles, they are spread across hundreds of square miles, with each circle measuring about 7 to 50 feet (2 to 15 m) across. So far, there has been no conclusive explanation for these circles. Some theories are that they are created by termites or are a result of the harsh, dry climate. As elsewhere, however, whenever there is an unexplained event, people also suspect alien activity.

Namibia's fairy circles are the cause of much debate.

Taken

A regular married couple, Barney and Betty Hill lived an ordinary life in Portsmouth, New Hampshire. Then one day, September 19, 1961, they were driving home from vacation. They claim they saw a craft hovering above their car. Then they saw strange "humanoids" looking at them from the craft's windows. Their last memory was that the spacecraft then descended to block their path. They were unable to remember anything that happened during the following hours, until they arrived home, confused.

The couple sensed that something strange had happened to them. Betty noticed unusual and unexplained stains on her dress. Their watches stopped working. There were circular marks on the underside of their car. When they placed a magnet near the marks, the magnet spun around.

The Hills were like any other couple until September 1961, when they drove home along a lonely road.

Under Hypnosis

Betty began to have nightmares about being on board a UFO, and Barney became unwell. A doctor suggested they see a **hypnotist**. While under hypnosis, the couple remembered details of their experience. They recalled being taken on board an alien craft where they were examined.

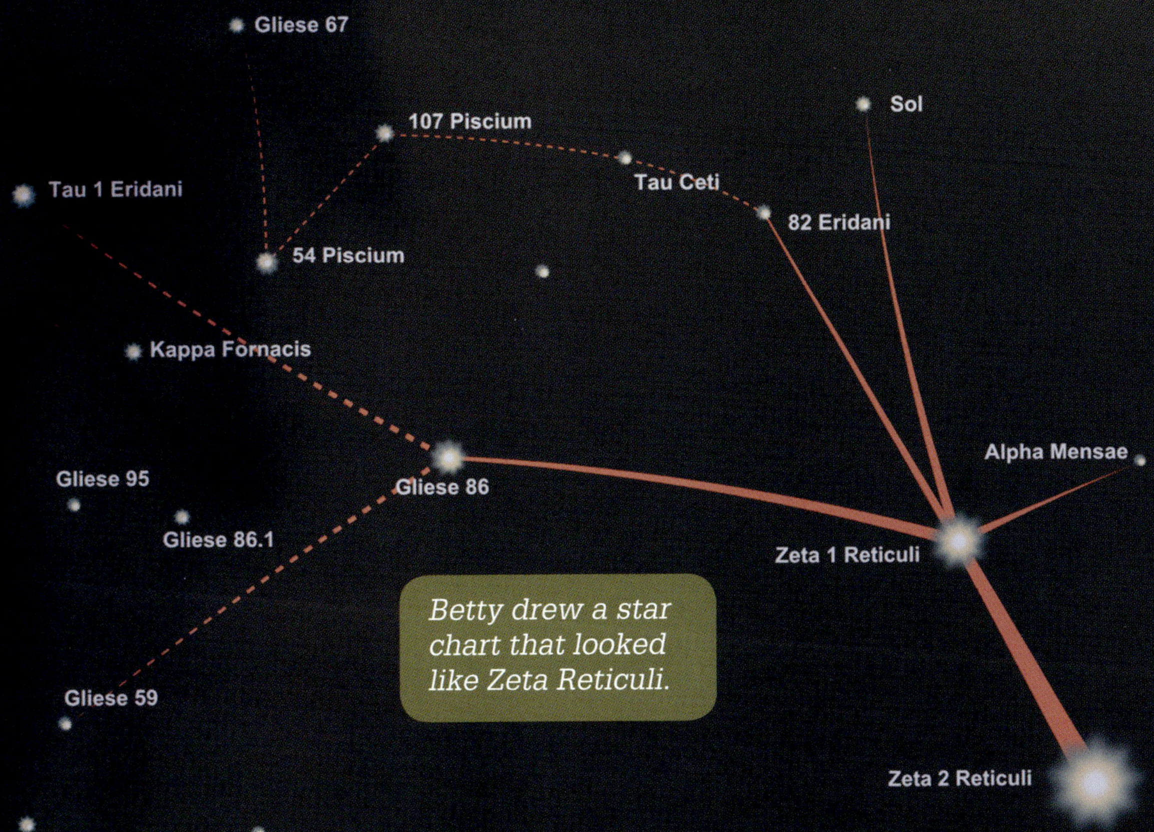

Betty drew a star chart that looked like Zeta Reticuli.

Barney and Betty reported the incident to Project Blue Book. They did not try to make money from their experience. They only talked about it after the story got picked up by a newspaper in 1965. For the rest of their lives, the couple continued to try to convince people about their alien abduction. Barney drew an image of an alien that has come to represent many of our ideas of what an alien looks like.

Betty said she had asked one of the aliens where they came from. On the basis of the reply, Betty drew a detailed sketch that seems similar to the star system Zeta Reticuli. Some people say this is proof Betty had communicated with aliens, as the star system was not discovered for another six years. Others say that it is coincidence.

Walton was working in the Apache National Forest.

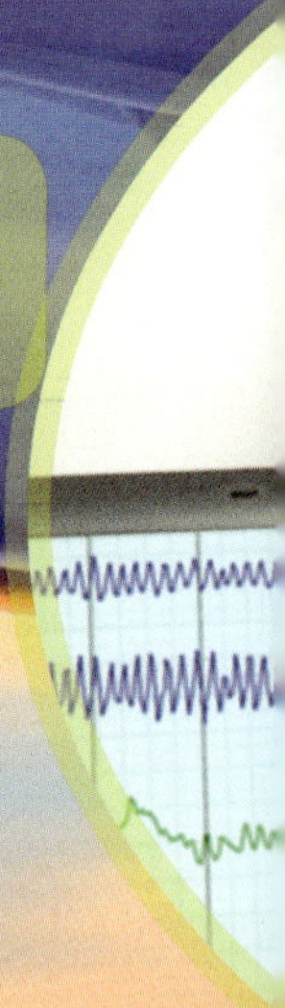

The Walton Case

On November 5, 1975, seven men were ending a day's work clearing logs in a forest in Arizona. They piled into a pickup truck. As they drove home, the men reported seeing a "luminous object, shaped like a flattened disk." According to the men, one of them, named Travis Walton, jumped out of the truck to take a better look. Suddenly, they said, he was struck down by a brilliant blue light. The other men were terrified, and drove off. One of them said he saw a glowing object rise off the ground. When they decided to go back and look for their friend, they could find no trace of him or the object they had seen.

Lie Detecting

The men reported the incident to the police, but a search revealed nothing. Five days later, Travis reappeared, with memories of aliens standing over him. The men took **lie detector tests**, which most of them passed. Some people claim the tests were not properly carried out. Was this an elaborate hoax, or was Travis really taken by aliens?

Travis Walton was soon famous. He wrote a book about his experience, which was made into a movie, *Fire in the Sky*, in 1993.

Alien at the Door!

According to a study carried out by the National Geographic Channel in 2012, more than a third of people in the United States believe aliens exist. More than 10 percent of the population believe they have seen an alien ship in the sky. Those who took part in the study revealed that 22 percent of them would try to make friends with an alien if one knocked on the door, 15 percent would run away, 13 percent would lock their door, and 2 percent would try to attack it!

Lie detectors measure changes in heart rate and breathing.

MYSTERY HUNTER

Based on the information you have read in this chapter, do you think there is enough evidence to prove that Travis or the Hills were abducted by aliens? Give reasons for your answer.

Chapter 5

LIFE BEYOND

Earth is the only planet we know that supports life. What makes it so special? Since the 1950s, humans have been exploring space, looking for signs of life beyond Earth. Astronomers, scientists, and astronauts have used remarkable advances in technology to collect evidence of the possibility of life beyond our world.

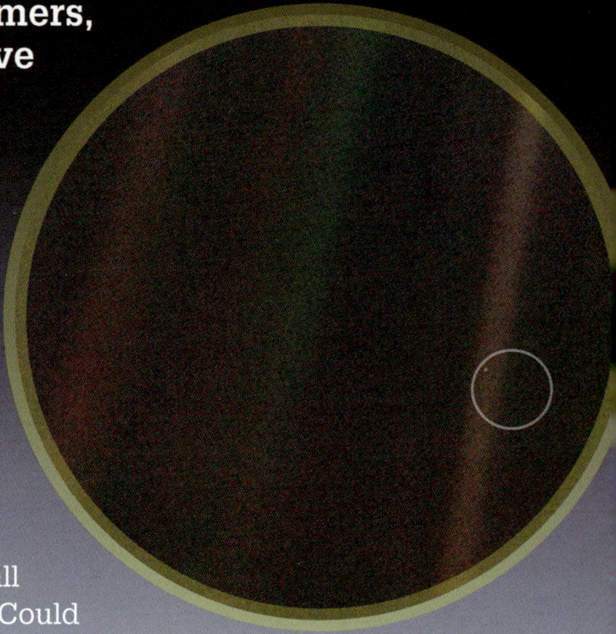

Dot of Light

An image taken by the *Voyager 1* spacecraft on February 14, 1990, from a distance of more than 4 billion miles (6 billion km) shows planet Earth as a tiny dot of light. Seen from outer space, Earth seems to be a very small part of the universe. Could other planets in the universe be home to other beings?

In this photo taken by Voyager 1, *Earth is just a dot. Feeling small?*

The Kepler space telescope has found hundreds of exoplanets.

"Habitable" Planets?

In the past 20 years, more than 3,000 exoplanets (planets orbiting other suns outside our solar system) have been discovered. Many of them were spotted by NASA's Kepler **space telescope**, which was launched into space in 2009. Forty of these planets are in the "**habitable** zone" of their sun, where the temperature is right for liquid water to exist. If it were too hot, the water would evaporate. If it were too cold, it would freeze. Liquid water is where life began on Earth, so could one of these planets also be home to life?

How Can We Tell?

Space telescopes like the NASA/ESA Hubble Space Telescope are on the lookout for signs of life on other planets. As well as measuring how hot or cold a planet is, they look for evidence that liquid water is plentiful, such as the presence of large amounts of water vapor in the planet's atmosphere. Then telescopes look for gases such as carbon dioxide, oxygen, and methane in a planet's atmosphere. These gases can be released into the air by living creatures. In 2008, Hubble discovered carbon dioxide in the atmosphere of a Jupiter-sized planet orbiting another sun. This planet was too hot for life to exist, but it was a good start.

Martian Life

The more we discover about space, the more people wonder about life on other planets. Instead of aliens coming to visit Earth, will humans discover life on other planets as we explore our own solar system and beyond? For centuries, people have wondered if Mars, the "Red Planet," could be home to extraterrestrials. It is known as the Red Planet because, through a telescope, it looks an orange–red color. Its color is caused by rust in its rocks. Mars is the fourth planet from the sun.

Looking for Life

In 1976, the first photos taken on the surface of Mars, by the *Viking 1* **lander**, were hazy. Today, our satellites, landers, and **rovers** send us highly detailed photos of the planet's surface. Mars has no visible signs of life at all. Its surface is rocky, barren, and dry. However, it looks as if water once ran freely on the planet, wearing down riverbeds and gullies. There is evidence that trickles of water still run on parts of the planet's surface today. Water is essential for life.

The Hubble Space Telescope took this photo of Mars in 2003.

In 2016, NASA's *Curiosity* rover, a six-wheeled buggy traveling through a depression named Gale Crater on Mars, detected further signs that Mars could support, or may have supported, life. It recorded "burps" of methane gas which may have been produced by **bacteria**. Most methane on Earth is produced as a waste gas by living organisms. However, *Curiosity* has tested many samples of the Martian soil. As yet, it has found no proof of any life.

Curiosity *took this "selfie" on the rocky planet.*

MYSTERIOUS FACTS

Could Mars support life today? Could it have supported life in the past? Consider these facts:

- The average temperature on Mars is -81 degrees Fahrenheit (-63° Celsius), which is similar to Antarctica. But scientists say the planet was warmer in the past.
- The atmosphere is 100 times thinner than on Earth, and is mostly made up of carbon dioxide rather than oxygen. But scientists believe the planet's atmosphere was much thicker in the past.
- Mars experiences violent storms that create thick clouds of dust for months on end.

Listen Up

A radio telescope is a large dish that collects radio waves from space. The dish focuses the waves on an antenna. A receiver takes the radio waves received by the antenna and turns them into electrical signals. A detector measures the electrical signal. A computer takes this data and creates an image from it. In this way, a picture of the sky can be created in radio waves. Many objects in far distant space cannot be seen in visible light, but they do send out radio waves. Radio telescopes are used to build up pictures of distant galaxies, but they are also used to listen for any radio signals, or messages, from other planets.

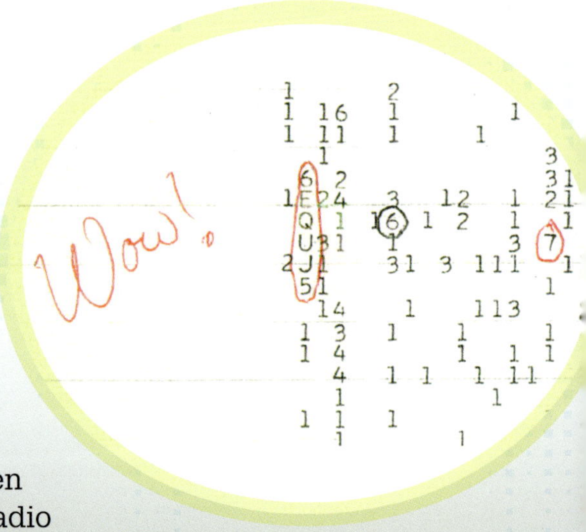

Wow!

Since the 1960s, radio telescopes have been listening for any pattern of radio waves that might be a signal from an alien civilization. After a long wait, in 1977 a radio telescope in the United States named Big Ear received an interesting signal. The careful pattern of the 72-second signal suggested that it might have been deliberately created by an intelligent being.

Here are the red marks that gave the Wow! signal its name.

These radio telescopes are in New Mexico.

It became known as the "Wow!" signal, because the scientist who spotted it, Jerry R. Ehman, circled it on his printout and wrote "Wow!" in red pen. The signal was traced to a cluster of stars in the constellation Sagittarius. Since the Wow! signal was picked up, scientists have tried to hear it again, using their most advanced telescopes. But so far, they have had no luck. Listen and wait!

Breakthrough Listen

In 2015, the space scientist Stephen Hawking (born 1942) said: "Somewhere in the cosmos, perhaps, intelligent life may be watching these lights of ours, aware of what they mean.... It's time to commit to finding the answer—to search for life beyond Earth. We are alive. We are intelligent. We must know." Hawking was launching a project named Breakthrough Listen, to further the hunt for alien signals using two powerful radio telescopes, the Green Bank Telescope in West Virginia, United States, and the Parkes Telescope in New South Wales, Australia. It is one of the biggest scientific searches for extraterrestrial life ever begun.

Stephen Hawking is behind the Breakthrough Listen project.

MYSTERY HUNTER

Based on the information you have read in this chapter, do you think that there is enough scientific evidence to prove that there is life on other planets? Do you think life will ever be detected on other planets? Give reasons for your answers.

Chapter 6

REVEALING INFORMATION

UFO-believers have accused governments across the world of trying to cover up the truth about aliens and UFOs. They think that governments have done this to avoid panic and unrest among the general public. However, other people argue that this makes little sense, because the lack of openness from governments has only created more mystery and actually led people to think there must be something to hide.

Why Cover Up?

If governments really have covered up evidence of UFOs or extraterrestrial beings coming to our planet, why would they do so? Humankind believes itself to be advanced above other animals on Earth. The discovery of alien beings might threaten that superior position. However, some people argue that there is no reason to fear that people would feel threatened. Since the earliest days, humans have believed in all-knowing spirits and gods.

Revealing the Truth?

In 2015, the U.S. government released thousands of documents about UFOs so that people could search them online. Taken from Project Blue Book, these include pictures claimed to be of UFOs and interviews with people who say they encountered extraterrestrial life from the 1940s to 1960s.

Should governments be more open about UFO reports?

Around the world, pressure is being put on governments to open up their UFO files to the public. In 2015, the UK's Ministry of Defense promised it would release top-secret documents about UFO sightings. It is believed the files will contain details of encounters such as the "Rendlesham Forest Incident," which took place in Suffolk, England, in 1980. According to stories, a U.S. airman named John Burroughs, who was stationed at an air base there, was exposed to radiation after a mystery "UFO visitation." Britain's Ministry of Defense has always maintained that the incident had nothing to do with UFOs.

Expert Opinion?

Richard Haines (born 1937) was once a scientist with NASA, working on programs such as the Apollo moon missions. After leaving NASA, he focused on documenting reports of UFO sightings and alien visits. He writes books, makes documentaries, and advises TV shows on UFOs. He has said: "I honestly don't know, but I'm trying to do my job and come to a rational answer based upon the evidence. I've come to the conclusion that there is quite an amount of good evidence suggesting intelligence behind the phenomenon [of UFOs]."

Some believe there are secrets behind the gates of the air base at Rendlesham.

The public cannot gain access to Area 51.

Area 51

For many years, people have talked about a top-secret place in the United States known as Area 51. There were many rumors but few facts. People claimed that Area 51 was a research center into alien activity and UFOs. Many believed it was in Nevada, inside an army training area that the public cannot enter. The secrecy surrounding the place only seemed to add to suspicions. Until 2013, the U.S. government would not even admit Area 51 existed.

The U-2 plane, designed to spy on the Soviet Union, was developed at Area 51.

Alien Rumors

Some people believe that the "crashed spacecraft" from Roswell is kept at Area 51, along with other evidence from the supposed alien landing. People have reported seeing UFOs in the sky above the Nevada base. Some believe that a sinister group of government agents known as the "Men in Black" is based at Area 51. The job of the Men in Black is to keep any alien or UFO sightings secret.

Are the Men in Black real or are they just in movies?

It Exists

In 2013, the Criminal Investigation Agency (CIA) finally admitted that Area 51 does, in fact, exist in Nevada. The CIA released papers and information about Area 51 and its activities. NASA's Major Charles Bolden said: "There is an Area 51. It's not what many people think... it's a normal research and development place. I never saw any aliens or alien spacecraft or anything when I was there. I think because of the secrecy of the aeronautics research that goes on there it's ripe for people to talk about aliens being there." Not everyone is convinced. Many people still believe Area 51's activities relate to alien research.

MYSTERIOUS FACTS

Here is what we know about Area 51:

- During World War II, the base was used as an airfield.
- President Dwight Eisenhower (1890–1969) allowed it to be used for developing the U-2 spy plane during the 1950s.
- Access is strictly limited.
- For a long time, Area 51 was left off maps. It is surrounded by desert. Areas where people could glimpse it were seized by the Air Force.

Hunting Answers

You have now read several reports of UFOs and alien sightings. These are just a selection of the hundreds of reports, most of them made in the past century. People have reported seeing bright creatures with glowing skin and odd-shaped bodies, traveling in bizarre spacecraft. They have reported abductions by aliens. Without conclusive proof, it is very hard to separate truth from fantasy. What can a mystery hunter do?

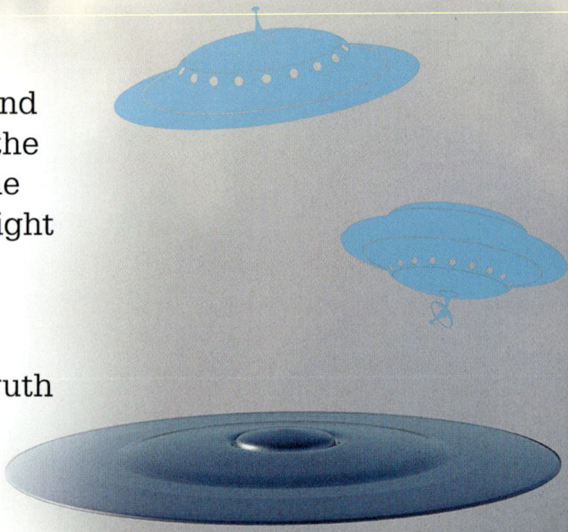

The Role of Hoaxers

The Internet has opened up great opportunities for people to easily and quickly share their experiences. A quick search on the Internet reveals some incredible claims about aliens and UFOs. Some seem very convincing until research reveals they are hoaxes. Such hoaxes make it even harder to believe the people who may be telling the truth. When people carry out successful hoaxes that convince some people or create doubt, they undermine the efforts of researchers to discover the reality about UFOs and aliens. Some people carry out hoaxes because it can be interesting to see how much nonsense people will believe. Others do it because they want to show how smart they are. Others do it to gain fame or money.

What is your conclusion: are aliens watching us?

Will a real UFO crash to Earth one day, proving that alien life does exist?

Can Technology Help Us?

Photographs seem to provide conclusive evidence of alien visits to Earth. However, as we have seen, these images can be faked even with household objects like string and light bulbs. Today it is possible to alter images using a computer: to know how realistic this is, just watch a Hollywood movie that shows dinosaurs running around! Faked images can be shared hundreds of thousands of times on the Internet, or shown across the world on TV stations.

Yet technology is also helping us to unpick the fact and fantasy behind aliens and UFOs. The more advances that we make exploring the mysterious world beyond our planet, the more we are likely to find conclusive evidence of other living beings, if they exist. There is nothing that will stop people from looking for answers to the unexplained.

MYSTERY HUNTER

When you come across an account of a UFO sighting, what process should you go through to decide whether or not the story might be true? Give reasons for your answer.

MYSTERY HUNTER ANSWERS

Chapter 1

Q *Consider the information you have read about the Nazca Lines. Do you think the Nazca Lines were created by humans or aliens? Justify your answer with historical evidence you have read in this book.*

A There is no evidence to suggest that aliens created these lines. Wooden sticks found by archaeologists suggest that the lines were made with simple tools. The most likely explanation is that they were made by local people, even though we do not know the purpose of their artworks.

Chapter 2

Q *Based on the evidence you have read, do you think the lights in Belgium were UFOs or something else? What scientific explanations can you give to back up your answer?*

A There is no conclusive evidence about what caused the sightings. Scientific evidence from the radar reports shows there was some activity in the air over Liège, but there is nothing to prove this was created by alien-built craft rather than human-built craft.

Chapter 3

Q *Using the information you have read in this chapter, decide if you think there is enough scientific and historical evidence to prove that aliens crashed their spaceship at Roswell. Give reasons for your answer.*

A There was evidence of a crash at Roswell, but the debris appeared to come from a weather balloon or, more probably, a surveillance balloon. There is no evidence to support a UFO crash. However, the army base at Roswell is very secretive. The sudden change in the army's account of what happened made people suspicious.

Chapter 4

Q *Based on the information you have read in this chapter, do you think there is enough evidence to prove that Travis or the Hills were abducted by aliens? Give reasons for your answer.*

A There is no conclusive evidence to decide one way or another about these claims. The Hills did not try to make money or gain fame from the incident. However, there is no scientific evidence to back up their account. Travis did gain both money and fame from his encounter. His claim is backed up by lie detector tests, but their results have been disputed.

Chapter 5

Q *Based on the information you have read in this chapter, do you think that there is enough scientific evidence to prove that there is life on other planets? Do you think life will ever be detected on other planets? Give reasons for your answers.*

A There is as yet no evidence that life exists or has existed on other planets. However, evidence obtained by space telescopes and rovers suggests that the conditions that made life possible on Earth may also exist on other planets. So far, the evidence from radio signals is uncertain. It would be reasonable to think that, given the number of possible habitable planets, we will one day discover evidence of some sort of life on other planets.

Chapter 6

Q *When you come across an account of a UFO sighting, what process should you go through to decide whether or not the story might be true? Give reasons for your answer.*

A When considering a new UFO sighting, you could ask the following questions: Who has made the claim and for what purpose? Has the evidence been examined by experts? Is there any other evidence to back up the claim, such as other witnesses or radar reports?

GLOSSARY

abducted kidnapped

archaeologists people who study the past through ruins and other remains

astronomers scientists who study space and the universe

atmosphere a blanket of gases surrounding a planet

atomic bombs very powerful explosive bombs that cause mass destruction

autopsy the process of cutting open a body to find out how it died

bacteria tiny living organisms

conclusive proving an argument

craft an aircraft or spaceship

debris broken pieces or remains of a wreck

dust devils whirlwinds

electromagnetic interference energy created by electrical and magnetic vibrations

evidence facts that confirm the truth about something

extraterrestrials beings that do not come from Earth

footage part of a film or movie

habitable suitable for life

headline a heading at the top of a newspaper

hoaxes tricks

hypnotist a person who can put someone under hypnosis, a sleep-like state that encourages a person to remember details of the past

lander a spacecraft designed to land on the surface of a planet or moon

lie detector tests tests that measure changes in heart rate and breathing caused by the stress of lying

medieval period the time between around AD 600 and 1500

optical illusion a trick of the eye

phenomenon (plural phenomena) a strange event, often unexplained

radar a system to detect the presence and speed of aircraft and other objects using radio waves

radio waves a type of electromagnetic wave that can travel through space

rovers robots designed to travel over the surface of another planet or moon

sound waves patterns caused by the movement of energy traveling away from a source of sound

space telescope a telescope in space that operates by remote control

surveillance observation of something

theory an idea that explains something

UFO (Unidentified Flying Object) a mysterious object in the sky

vision something seen in a dream or trance, usually as part of an intense spiritual experience

waterspouts tornadoes over water

weather balloon a balloon that carries equipment to study conditions high in the atmosphere

FOR MORE INFORMATION

BOOKS

Levete, Sarah. *Science Fact or Fiction? You Decide!* New York, NY: Crabtree, 2010.

Milner Halls, Kelly, and Rick C. Spears. *Alien Investigation: Searching for the Truth About UFOs and Aliens.* Minneapolis, MN: Millbrook Press, 2012.

Polydoros, Lori. *Top 10 UFO and Alien Mysteries* (Top 10 Unexplained). North Mankato, MN: Capstone Press, 2012.

Steer, D. (editor). *Alienology* (Ologies). Somerville, MA: Candlewick Press, 2010.

WEBSITES

Discover more about NASA's research into planets beyond our solar system:
exoplanets.jpl.nasa.gov

Do some more research on UFO sightings:
kidskonnect.com/science/ufo

Find out what the ESA has to say about life on other planets:
www.esa.int/esaKIDSen/SEMXWOSTGOF_LifeinSpace_0.html

Explore the NASA website for photographs and facts about other worlds:
www.nasa.gov

INDEX